FIREFIGHTER HEROES

SMOKE JUMPERS

By Spencer Brinker

Consultant: Beth Gambro
Reading Specialist, Yorkville, Illinois

Minneapolis, Minnesota

Teaching Tips

Before Reading

- Look at the cover of the book. Discuss the picture and the title.
- Ask readers to brainstorm a list of what they already know about firefighters. What can they expect to see in the book?
- Go on a picture walk, looking through the pictures to discuss vocabulary and make predictions about the text.

During Reading

- Read for purpose. Encourage readers to think about what smoke jumpers do as they are reading.
- Ask readers to look for the details of the book. What are they learning about how smoke jumpers put out fires?
- If readers encounter an unknown word, ask them to look at the sounds in the word. Then, ask them to look at the rest of the page. Are there any clues to help them understand?

After Reading

- Encourage readers to pick a buddy and reread the book together.
- Ask readers to name two things smoke jumpers do during a fire. Find the pages that tell about these things.
- Ask readers to write or draw something they learned about smoke jumpers.

Credits
Cover and title page, © Hemis/Alamy Stock Photo and © F.C.G./Adobe Stock; 3, © Frazao Studio Latino/iStock; 5, © Piligrim/Shutterstock; 7, © Toa55/iStock; 8–9, © U.S. Department of the Interior/Wikimedia Commons; 10, © costasss/iStock; 11, © Brad Simmons/Adobe Stock; 13, © standret/Adobe Stock and © sjessup/Adobe Stock; 14–15, © Region 5 Photography/Creative Commons Attribution 2.0 Generic; 16–17, © Kaibab National Forest/Creative Commons Attribution-Share Alike 2.0 Generic; 19, © amriphoto/iStock; 20–21, © BLM Photo / Alamy Stock Photo; 22, © lovelyday12/Adobe Stock, © Sven Taubert/Adobe Stock, and © Brad Simmons/Adobe Stock; 23TL, © photocdn6/iStock; 23TM, © US National Interagency Fire Center/Wikimedia Commons; 23TR, © da-kuk/iStock; 23BL, © Pacific Southwest Region 5/Creative Commons Attribution 2.0 Generic; 23BM, © Brad Simmons/Adobe Stock; 23BR, © Toa55/iStock.

See BearportPublishing.com for our statement on Generative AI Usage.

Library of Congress Cataloging-in-Publication Data

Names: Brinker, Spencer, author.
Title: Smoke jumpers / by Spencer Brinker.
Description: Minneapolis, Minnesota : Bearport Publishing Company, [2025] |
Series: Firefighter heroes | Includes bibliographical references and
index.
Identifiers: LCCN 2024022436 (print) | LCCN 2024022437 (ebook) | ISBN
9798892327206 (library binding) | ISBN 9798892327701 (paperback) | ISBN
9798892328074 (ebook)
Subjects: LCSH: Smokejumpers--Juvenile literature. | Wildfire fighters--Juvenile literature.
Classification: LCC SD421.23 .B73 2025 (print) | LCC SD421.23 (ebook) |
DDC 634.9/618--dc23/eng/20240516
LC record available at https://lccn.loc.gov/2024022436
LC ebook record available at https://lccn.loc.gov/2024022437

For more information, write to Bearport Publishing, 5357 Penn Avenue South, Minneapolis, MN 55419.

Contents

A Forest Fire

There are **flames** and smoke.

Trees are burning.

The forest is on fire!

We need smoke jumpers!

The fire is moving fast.

But there are no roads to get there.

Smoke jumpers are special firefighters.

They can do the job.

The firefighter heroes pull on **jumpsuits**.

They put **parachutes** on their backs.

Then, they rush to an airplane.

NATIONAL INTERAGENCY FIRE CENTER
Boise, Idaho
N990BH
RAMP SERVICES
Say parachute like PAIR-uh-shoots
Parachute

The plane takes the heroes close to the fire.

It is time for the firefighters to jump.

Whoosh!

The parachutes slow their fall.

The smoke jumpers land safely.

The plane drops tools.

Food and water come down, too.

Sometimes, the heroes will be in the forest for days.

The heroes get to work!

They use axes to cut down plants.

This makes a big path.

The fire cannot go across it.

Some **wildfires** move very fast.

The heroes can be in danger.

They may not be able to get away.

Fire shelters keep them safe.

E-633
Fire shelter

Smoke jumpers work as a team.

On the ground, heroes help one another.

Sometimes, planes drop **chemicals** from above.

Smoke jumpers stop wildfires.

This keeps plants and animals safe.

The heroes work hard to save forests.

Thanks, firefighters!

STIHL

Smoke Jumper Tools

Smoke jumpers need special tools to stop wildfires.

Glossary

chemicals human-made things that are sometimes used to put out fires

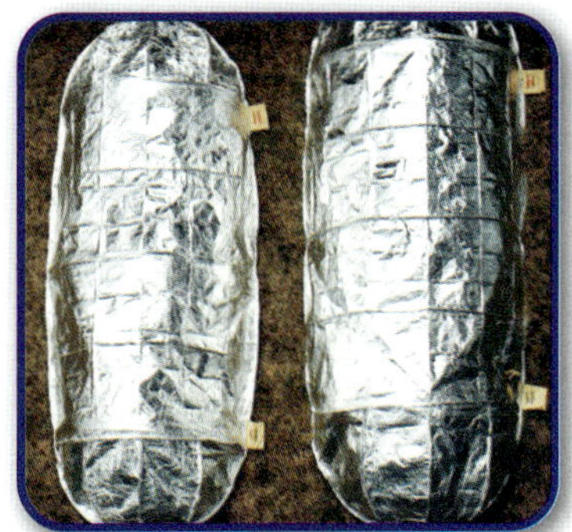

fire shelters special bags that keep people safe in a fire

flames the glowing, moving parts of fires

jumpsuits clothing that covers the whole body

parachutes cloth that slow down falling objects

wildfires fires that destroy large areas in nature

Index

Read More

Murray, Julie. *Smokejumpers (Fierce Jobs)*. Minneapolis: Abdo Zoom, 2021.

Suen, Anastasia. *Wildfires (Extreme Weather)*. Mankato, MN: Amicus Ink, 2021.

Learn More Online

1. Go to **FactSurfer.com** or scan the QR code below.
2. Enter "**Firefighter Smoke Jumpers**" into the search box.
3. Click on the cover of this book to see a list of websites.

About the Author

Spencer Brinker lives in Minnesota with his family, dog, and lizard.